Sparks of a Wallflower

C. Olsson

BookLeaf Publishing

India | USA | UK

Presentation by *BookLeaf Publishing*

Web: www.bookleafpub.com

E-mail: info@bookleafpub.com

ISBN: 9789358316346

First edition 2024

To those who have always been more wallflowers and never felt like anyone understands them, you will find someone who helps you find your spark and turn your shards into a beautiful masterpiece...

ACKNOWLEDGEMENT

I want to start by thanking my friend Haley, who sparked my love for writing with creating an Instagram account during the COVID-19 shut down and helped design artwork that went with my poems and musings and my friends for their unwavering support. I want to thank the experiences I went through for turning me into the person I am today. I also want to thank my significant other for giving me my spark back and being my safe heaven, he is my home. I want to thank my parents for giving me the life I have, and my soul dog, for loving me unconditionally. In addition, thank you to the kids I have worked with over the last 6 years, who have taught me how to look at things differently and gave me a purpose. To you, the reader, for giving me a chance. I hope something resonated with you and you could find comfort or understanding in at least one of these poems. Lastly, I want to thank BookLeaf Publishing for this opportunity to publish my work.

PREFACE

Everything that I am today has been the result of what I have experienced. As I have gotten older, I realized that my feelings towards those experiences are completely valid, but they also have changed how I look at them. The poems in this book portray those changes: from feeling insignificant and trying to find something to hold onto to feel safe, to finding that spark that I lost a long time ago and being stronger than what broke me. I saw a quote that resonated with me a few years ago that said, "Be the person you needed when you were younger". I live everyday making that quote my life and how I portray myself. I have come a long way than the insecure girl mentioned in some of the poems, and hope that I have become the woman she needed for others.

My Childhood

It started with barely
a flickering tremble of the eyes -
now its debilitating.
Reducing my brain into nullity,
the seizures took away my childhood.

Saints

From the countless anxiety ridden nights - to the daily medications and monitoring, my family are saints who deserve all the best in life.

Seizure

The dog
flicker flicker drop
street.

Laughter

I answered a question
wrong - it's the end of the
world. I can still feel the heat
from the redness on my cheeks;
the laughter still ringing
through my ears.
And the tears are still welled behind
my eyes.

Invisible

Withdrawing farther
and farther into myself
was a calming solstice
where I could be free
from hurt and believe
everything would be ok...
eventually.

Kintsukaroi

She picked up the
broken pieces,
glued them together
with gold, and
shone brighter
than ever before.

Numb

It doesn't hurt anymore. The feeling
of betrayal. The loss. The pain.
Developing a tolerance to it,
I became numb.

Don't Cry

Her eyes sparkled,
tears threatening to spill over.
Don't cry.
Don't show them you're hurt.
Don't cry.
Don't show them you're scared.
Don't cry.
You're okay. You'll be okay.
Sometime, this will just be a memory.

Labrinyth

My mind is like a
labyrinth with all these
thoughts swirling around.
Rifling through them is like
flipping through a textbook for
an answer with no table of contents.

Birthday

I never really enjoyed
it. Not only did I get
the most perfect family -
I was also abandoned by
the ones who were
supposed to never
leave.

Abandonment

Maybe that was why
I have abandonment issues.
The ones who were supposed
to take of care and love me
unconditionally, threw me away.

Mixed Feelings

I was always angry.
Taking it out on
the wrong set of parents.
Knowing I was adopted
for a better life, but why
didn't you at least try?
Knowing you loved me
so much you gave me away
to someone who could take
that love and provide for me
in ways you couldn't.

When death comes knocking

I was too young to
understand what death meant.
I was too young to understand that
I was never going to see you again.
Each year the pain gets worse and
worse. All the missed birthdays
and holidays and life events that you
should be there for. What I would give to
be able to run into your arms again and
feel your heartbeat one last time.
I love you.

Rosy Cheeks

Your twinkling eyes and
distinct Boston accent when
you said "deah" after our name
will be remembered always
but not as much as the memory
of your bright rosy cheeks.

Sweden

Karaste. Karlek. Mysa. Lykke.
These are words I have had
to learn on my own and figure
out how to pronounce. But their
meanings... I have all learned
from you.

Karaste

Cara "deah", have you had
enough to eat "deah", I love
you "deah". I would do anything
to hear that word coming from
you again.

Karlek

Love.
Love from a parent or
from a pet. Love from a
grandparent or from a
friend. Love from family or
from a significant other.
Love for the little things.
There is nothing more
powerful than the feeling
of love.

Mysa

Cozy.
The feeling of the sand
between your toes, saltwater
in your hair. The feeling of
being curled up under a blanket
with a dog by the fire.
Cozy.

Lykke

Happiness.
A nice breeze blowing
through your hair mixed
with salty air. The wagging
of a tail at high speed, and
the sounds of laughter
ringing through your ears.
Happiness.

Some people are worth melting for

Your voice sounds
like how
a warm hug feels.

Thank you for being that someone

Do you ever just look at someone
and see your future in their eyes?
Are you ever touched by someone
and feel your broken pieces
being melded together? Do you
ever just sit with someone and realize
that you are safe?
You gave me my spark back. You gave
me my childhood laughter back.
I could never never thank you enough.

www.ingramcontent.com/pod-product-compliance
Lightning Source LLC
LaVergne TN
LVHW050505210726
843509LV00015BA/3000